Bringing the
Social
Media
#Revolution
to Health Care

Mayo Clinic Center for Social Media

"*The great contribution we can make is to prepare the oncoming generations to think that they can and will think for themselves.*"

— Charles H. Mayo

"*We think of truth as something that is invariable, but add a new circumstance and we have a new truth.*"

— William J. Mayo

Contents

Foreword

A century ago, the medical establishment considered William J. Mayo, M.D. (Dr. Will) and Charles H. Mayo, M.D. (Dr. Charlie) radicals. When they created the first integrated group practice of medicine, many saw it as an evasion of personal responsibility. A physician, conventional wisdom held, should take complete responsibility for his (and it almost always was his) patients.

Dr. Will and Dr. Charlie saw it differently. They knew medical knowledge was developing faster than any individual could master. And they realized that if patients had to rely on a single doctor, their care wouldn't be as good as what a team of specialists could provide.

That same radical spirit is behind what Mayo Clinic is doing today—helping to lead the social media revolution in health care.

Dr. Will explained the brothers' perspective in his commencement address at Rush Medical College in Chicago in 1910:

> "As we grow in learning, we more justly appreciate our dependence upon each other. The sum-total of medical knowledge is now so great and wide-spreading that it would be futile for one man to attempt to acquire, or for any one man to assume that he has, even a good working knowledge of any large part of the world. The very necessities of the case are driving practitioners into cooperation. *The best interest of the patient is the only interest to be considered,* and in order that the sick may have the benefit of advancing knowledge, *union of forces is necessary.*"

More than a century ago, the Mayo brothers' first partner, Dr. Henry Plummer, developed the unified medical record, an extremely powerful internal networking tool, to pool specialists' knowledge to best serve patients.

Dr. Will and Dr. Charlie were outwardly focused as well. They were the original social networkers in medicine. For six months of the year, one would stay in Rochester, Minnesota, caring for patients, while the other traveled to teach and to learn. Then, they'd switch.

They saw this outreach as crucial to providing the best care to every patient, every day. The Mayo brothers felt obligated to advance medical science and share innovations so others could apply them. And while medicine at the turn of the 20th century was male-dominated, the need to provide the best care possible meant growing the Mayo practice to embrace inclusiveness and diversity.

Mayo Clinic has a legacy of leadership in medicine. Today, Mayo Clinic is among the leaders in using social media to support health and health care.

We created the Mayo Clinic Center for Social Media to explore how social tools can improve patient care, catalyze medical research, strengthen medical education and promote continuous professional development. These commitments serve to shape the quickly-growing Social Media Health Network of organizations around the world.

We approach this with humility. Like Dr. Will and Dr. Charlie we know we can't do it alone.

We see our role as catalyst and clearinghouse. We're actively developing practical social media applications, and hope others can learn from our experience. The field is growing rapidly, with innovations arising all over the world. We want to help spread the best ideas.

Dr. Will and Dr. Charlie created the first integrated group practice of medicine and the medical record to facilitate it. Their innovation spread around the world largely because of their old-fashioned social networking facilitated by trains and boats.

As stewards of their legacy and early adopters of modern social networking tools, we see an opportunity and feel a responsibility to help the broader health care system harness social tools safely and effectively.

A key phrase in Dr. Will's address to Rush Medical College has become our Mayo Clinic motto: "The best interest of the patient is the only interest to be considered."

And this is what drives our Center for Social Media and Social Media Health Network. It's not about competitive advantage. It's about patients, and how these tools can help us serve them better... and work with them for their health.

We're committed to helping our colleagues around the world who want to learn—*from* us and *with* us—how to apply these revolutionary tools fight disease, promote health, and improve health care.

> John H. Noseworthy, M.D.
> *President and CEO*
> *Mayo Clinic*

Preface

We're right in the middle of a definitive paradigm shift in health care. In particular, we're seeing a growing need for, and growing expectation of, two-way engagement between patients and providers at every stage of the care trajectory.

This trajectory of care is wide ranging. It includes conversations between providers and patients that generate shared decisions about medication and treatment choices; monthly meetings of Mayo Clinic's Patient-Family Advisory Council to provide input for protocols such as our hospital discharge summary; and providers who gather their patients' family, friends, and spiritual support network to share their loved one's journey to health. This care trajectory includes, of course, the greatest challenge we all face—redesigning our health care system.

The value of engaging in clear, open, two-way communication at every point of care has become abundantly clear. Active engagement between providers and patients, along with their caregivers, has a demonstrably profound impact on patient and provider satisfaction, patient compliance, and improved clinical outcomes. Social media is helping to make much of this constructive engagement happen. These real-time tools are allowing patients to express their interests and needs at every point along the care trajectory. Social media allows individual providers and those serving in large medical care systems like Mayo Clinic to join the conversation beyond constraints of time or geography.

My primary goal as the Medical Director of the Mayo Clinic Center for Social Media is to foster these critical conversations to enhance the real value of health care for our patients and their families and for our providers and staff. As Mahatma Gandhi famously said, "We must become the change we want to see in the world."

When it comes to changing health care, I say we must crowd-source the change we want to see in the world. Social media allows that to happen, and *Bringing the Social Media Revolution to Health Care* is a guide to doing so.

Farris Timimi, M.D.
Medical Director
Mayo Clinic Center for Social Media

Acknowledgements

Bringing the Social Media Revolution to Health Care simultaneously encapsulates our experience at Mayo Clinic and offers a broader call to action for the future. Crucial contributions from so many have catalyzed our Mayo Clinic progress. Recognizing their roles is not only right; hopefully it also will inspire and encourage their peers in other institutions to be similarly supportive.

Twelve years ago our Public Affairs leaders, particularly John LaForgia and Chris Gade, created and built support for our Mayo Clinic syndicated TV program, *Medical Edge*, which created a reservoir of quality content we could tap for our efforts. Five years later, they recognized the potential of "new media" and encouraged our experimentation.

That support would not have been effective, however, without buy-in from our front-line Public Affairs colleagues, who moved fairly quickly from eye rolling about blogging and tweeting to enthusiastically embracing social media tools to do their work more effectively.

Our Mayo Clinic IT and legal departments, instead of blocking access and erecting obstacles, provided guidance and support for safe and effective social media. Dan Goldman's support as our legal counsel has made all the difference, as he focuses on managing benefits as well as risks.

Jim Hodge and Dr. Victor Montori inspired us to think bigger, as did our Mayo Clinic CEO, Dr. John Noseworthy, and our Chief Administrative Officer, Shirley Weis. Without their advocacy the Mayo Clinic Center for Social Media would not exist.

Many from outside of Mayo Clinic also have made major contributions. Shel Holtz and Andy Sernovitz provided perspective from other industries at the right time to help us maintain momentum. Ragan Communications has worked with us to produce numerous educational webinars and in-person conferences. And our External Advisory Board members bring practical experience and thought leadership, which you'll see in the following pages.

Special thanks to Meredith Gould, Ph.D., whose expertise and good-natured tenacity as the project manager and editor for this volume has made its publication a reality.

On behalf of the Mayo Clinic Center for Social Media, we hope you will find these essays encouraging and inspiring, and that you will join us in the revolution.

Lee Aase   Farris Timimi, M.D.
Director   *Medical Director*

Section One

Getting Inspired

Health care Social Media Is About Passion

Patricia F. Anderson
@PFAnderson
Taubman Health Sciences Library
University of Michigan-Ann Arbor

I don't know about other people, but for me, social media in health care is about passion. It's about stories and storytelling. It's about reaching out, being a support, answering questions, and getting answers to my own questions. It's about sharing, observing, learning, humility, friendship, discovery, and surprise.

When I started using Twitter and Facebook, those aspects of social media were completely opaque to me. Simply said, I did *not* understand. It's hard for people to believe now, but when I first began using Twitter, all I did was post my current location, like Foursquare now, but without pictures. I wasn't cute or clever about it. I was boring. People still followed me, which was incredibly baffling.

The experience of a social media platform not "making sense" when you first start is fairly typical. Get started. Try it out. Learn how things work. Watch what other people do. Ask for help. One of two things will happen.

Sooner or later a "light bulb" experience will occur, an *Aha*! moment when the tool or platform begins making sense and you see the value. Ask around, and people will share their stories of when it began making sense to them. The alternative? The *Aha*! moment doesn't happen in a reasonable amount of time and you give up. The trick is giving it a sincere, fair trial; sometimes that's easier said than done.

I've found each social media tool seems to attract communities of interest in different topics. My own interests are so diverse that I find valuable communities almost everywhere. For most people, the greatest challenge is finding those communities. This presents as a problem in at least two ways:

1. Where do your people "live"? For your topics and communities of interest, what tools are the ones they find most useful?
2. Once you have an account in a tool or service, how do you find people who interest you?

Note: Just because you haven't found them doesn't mean your people aren't there, and searching popular topics is a better way to find spammers than anyone you'd really want to know.

While social media engagement has proven its worth in my life many times and in many ways, the real reasons I'm there (which I listed at the beginning) aren't always persuasive to colleagues who look for more tangible outcomes.

Here are some concrete benefits that have come directly from my engagement with social media: co-authorship on research articles, speaker invitations, keynote invitations, being placed on campus-wide advisory committees, consulting opportunities, and unique research datasets. Membership on the External Advisory Board for the Mayo Clinic Center for Social Media is far from the least of these.

Gear Up for Change That's Already Here

Ed Bennett
@EdBennett
University of Maryland Medical Center

My passion for social media was sparked by two events separated by ten years. During the late 1990s, back when the commercial Web began, I helped dozens of organizations develop their first Web presence.

Many business leaders understood the radical changes a Web site could bring, but they were in the minority before 1999. Most belittled the idea, sticking with business as usual. (*"Our customers use the yellow pages."*) Sadly, the most skeptical industry was health care. Some major hospitals didn't have a Web site until 2006.

The second event was more personal—watching my daughter grow up with texting, MySpace, and then Facebook becoming the glue holding her friends together.

As I explored these services two things became clear, and by 2008 I was convinced that:

1. Social media was redefining the Web, providing tools people wanted and were using at extraordinary rates. It wasn't going away and it seemed to be in the early stages of something big.
2. Hospitals would, once again, stay behind.

That's what motivated me in 2009 to build the Hospital Social Network List. A tool for hospital marketing communications (aka, marcomm) folks, it answered the critical management question, *"You want our hospital to be on Facebook? Is anyone else doing it?"*

Three years later, a significant percentage of hospitals are active on social media and are just starting to understand the value for our patients, community, and organizations.

These trends are now converging within the health care industry:

1. Workforce demographics: Staff who grew up with social media are getting into more senior management positions.
2. Patient expectations: Patients use these social media to connect with hospitals and health care professionals for themselves and families.
3. Patient communities: Empowered patients use social media to take charge of their own health and encourage others to do the same.

How can you prepare for these changes?

1. Learn these tools and become comfortable with communities they build.
2. Prepare your organization for change. Educate and encourage the participation of your peers and management.
3. Health care has hundreds of topics and/or areas: what's your special interest? Find your niche and become knowledgeable and passionate.
4. Build a network of trusted colleagues beyond your organization. Share ideas, answer questions, and don't be afraid to ask for advice. (You are always welcome to call me—the telephone is still my favorite social media tool.)

Most of all, have fun! There's a reason more than 900 million people use Facebook.

Social Media for Health Care Makes Sense

Chris Boyer
@ChrisBoyer
Inova Health System

I have always disliked hospitals. My early memories included scary emergency rooms and sharp needles (I was pretty sick as a kid). At 18, I nearly died and spent two weeks in the hospital (over Christmas, New Year's, and my birthday).

I vaguely remember nurses and doctors being kind and compassionate, honestly trying to help me and my parents understand what was happening. But I was sick and scared, and I still can't remember clearly. When I left the hospital feeling better, I remember trying really hard to forget that experience and to do whatever it took to never go back into a hospital.

Except for the fact that I now work for a hospital, my experience is not unique. Many people don't think about hospitals until they absolutely have to, and then it's coming from a perspective of fear. I'm certain that when people think of hospitals, they're inclined to speak in hushed whispers or say prayers under their breath. People don't like hospitals.

What does this have to do with social media?

Before social media became so popular, hospitals would spend time communicating and marketing in traditional ways—through broadcast, one-way messages. And people (like my family and others) would be forced to swallow whatever was being fed to them.

It wasn't natural. Health is a personal thing.

Each and every one of us is personally invested in our health. So there we were as patients, terrified by our experiences, lost in the confusion of health care, and blindly following orders from health care marketers. No wonder this wasn't working. Traditional marketing strategies and tools just aren't effective health care.

Social media has leveled the proverbial playing field. Now patients can communicate about health at any time. They can share fears over ill-fated diagnoses with distant friends and families. They can connect with people across the world who struggle with similar health conditions, finding support and companionship. They can question whether the doctor gave the right diagnosis or express displeasure at having to sit in a waiting room (that smells like urine) for hours.

Social media is natural for patients.

What can we, as health care communicators, learn from this? Simply: patients use social media because they can—and should. It's a way of dealing with the difficult and bloated process of "health care." If we're going to succeed as social media communicators, we need to:

- Be helpful. Often patients turn to social media because they're scared (and need social support) or confused (because your Web site is a mess and the phone operators at your hospital don't have correct information).
- Give patients the opportunity to weigh in on care experiences. If they complain, listen and address the concern quickly.
- Refrain from broadcasting and marketing. Share information patients and caregivers will find valuable and useful. Don't use confusing clinical speak; share interesting relevant information.
- Go with your instincts. Social media sites grow and thrive organically. You'll know when it's working and when it's not. And don't be afraid to fail—social media is pretty forgiving.

Social media in health care makes sense—for patients and for us.

Social Media Starts With People

Shel Holtz
@shelholtz
Holtz Communication + Technology

In the earliest days of the Internet's life as a public medium, I interviewed interface guru Jared Spool for an article. Spool, who runs a consultancy called User Interface Engineering, told me that technology—*any* technology—can do only three things:

1. Solve a problem.
2. Make an existing process better.
3. Allow you to do something unimaginable before the technology was introduced.

If you're not doing one of these three things with a Web site, Spool said it makes sense to ask, why are you putting it on the Web?

The same rule applies to social media. If you're new to it, you may want to jump in because your competitors are doing it, because it's cool and you don't want to be *un*cool, or because your boss told you to use it.

How you actually use social media, though, should be based on problems you can solve, processes you can improve, and ways you can deliver value to people that simply didn't exist before. Think of it, as Clay Shirky does in his book, *Cognitive Surplus,* like electricity. Nobody uses electricity for its own sake. We use electricity because it can light our homes, power our televisions, and let us open cans of fruit cocktail without risking carpal tunnel syndrome (or a nasty cut).

Your audience uses social media for these exact same reasons. YouTube videos provide quick bursts of information or entertainment (or, ideally, both). Interactions on Facebook can produce personal gratification (from seeing photos from your brother's family vacation, for instance), answers to questions, a sense of belonging to a community, or the satisfaction of accomplishment (if the community to which you belong sets a goal and completes a task).

Thus, your introduction to social media shouldn't be about tools you can use or even which tools are most commonly used among peers. It should be about what the people you're trying to reach are going through, what would make life better, and how you might use social platforms and channels to accomplish these things.

On the other hand, from studying how patients, families, staff, and other stakeholders use social channels and platforms other hospitals make available, you can develop a strong sense of how they serve to solve problems, improve processes, and/or let these audiences do things that weren't previously possible.

To put it succinctly, effective use of social media starts with the people who will be using it. If that's where *you* begin, you won't go wrong.

<u>Notes</u>

Section Two

Being Strategic

Seven Thoughts on Social Media Strategy

Lee Aase
@LeeAase
Mayo Clinic Center for Social Media

1. *Start from business priorities and goals.* Social media isn't something to do for its own sake or because the tools are shiny and new. Think about what you were hired to do or needs you see in your organization and how these tools can help. In my case, social tools supported our media relations, my first job at Mayo Clinic.
2. *Become personally familiar with the tools.* Develop deep familiarity with basic social media platforms by using them. Set up personal accounts before creating any for your employer to help you see how to best apply them for work.
3. *Start by watching and listening.* Listen to what others say about your organization. Watch how others use the tools.
4. *Ask for help.* People in online communities are generally welcoming of new members, particularly those who approach with a sense of humility.
5. *Pay attention to community norms.* If you watch and listen and approach online connections with humility, it's unlikely you'll become "that guy." Don't act in ways wildly outside community norms for a community if you want to become a trusted member.
6. *Don't be snowed by the purists.* My friend Andy Sernovitz talks about "bloggers who blog about blogging," for whom any deviation from what they consider the "right" way to engage online is viewed with contempt. They aren't your audience. Don't let purists' opinions keep you from doing what's right for your situation and organization.
7. *Planning is more important than plans.* Think about priorities and why you're engaging in social media, but keep the planning horizon short. Plan early. Plan often. Lather. Rinse. Repeat. The content of any plan isn't as important as the thought process that informed its development. Our Mayo Clinic Center for Social Media works on a 100-day planning cycle. Don't be afraid of having a similarly short planning cycle.

Strategy in social media isn't appreciably different from other types of business strategy. You'll address the same questions: What resources do I have? What tools are available? What could I accomplish with additional resources? Still, here's one key way social media business strategy is different:

Altruism pays. Social tools have dramatically reduced the cost of sharing knowledge, and the resulting relationships can be much more valuable than the knowledge itself. Keep costs low and you'll be amazed at the benefits you'll realize from sharing freely.

Seven Common-Sense Techniques for Building a Good Strategy

Chris Boyer
@ChrisBoyer
Inova Health System

Remember this: Social media tools are designed to augment already existing ways people communicate. And this: A good social media strategy always relies heavily on common sense.

1. *Get started and get familiar.* Jump in and play with social media. The more time you spend with social media, the more you'll understand how these tools facilitate communication. Pick up the nuances of online communities—how people interact and share ideas.

    Common-sense tip: If you're afraid to run your own personal Twitter or Facebook page, you may not be the right person to run one for your business.

2. *Think about how these tools can be used for business.* It's one thing to use social media to socialize. Now, start thinking about how your organization can participate in a credible way. Throw away all traditional biases and figure out ways to connect with your audience that are meaningful to them and your business.

    Common-sense tip: Using social media for business is slightly different than using it for yourself; but remember, people appreciate businesses that speak in a "human voice."

3. *Create something worth following.* As you build your social media presence, create a communication strategy that focuses on meaningful, relevant content. Include content that you and medical experts create as well as content from other sources.

    Common-sense tip: People don't really care about DaVinci robots and quality awards. They simply want to trust that you're the best health care provider. Focus on building trust.

4. *Build a network of peers.* Social media use constantly changes and evolves. It's hard to keep abreast of the latest developments. The good news is that we're all in the same boat. And since we all use social media, we've built a tight-knit community, and many of us like to share our experiences. Network with others involved in the MCCSM, as well as other online communities.

Common-sense tip: Having a network of peers not only helps you learn from others, it can also provide a valuable emotional support network when you might be struggling.

5. *Align efforts with business strategies.* As you gain knowledge about how social media can be used for business, start aligning the tools to meet your business goals. Social media can be used effectively for building brand, developing communities of interest, and supporting growth goals. Develop a separate strategy for each business goal that utilizes social media.

Common-sense tip: Don't try to use every social media platform for each strategy; it's better to choose the right tools for the right strategy.

6. *Measure what you're doing.* Keep track of how your social media strategies are performing. Develop a list of success measurements (i.e., key performance indicators [KPIs]) you can monitor and track. Measure regularly and then honestly review the results to refine your strategies.

Common-sense tip: Don't forget we're doing this for business reasons—if you can't report on the measurements of your success, you run the risk of letting your successor do it better.

7. *Share successes and learn from failures.* When you have a success, share it openly with others in your organization and peers online. We all like to celebrate when something goes right. On the other hand, when you don't succeed, learn from those moments to help improve your efforts going forward.

Common-sense tip: The cost to start a social media strategy is far less than the cost for traditional media efforts; failure is sometimes OK, but by all means, do what's right for the patients.

Social media is now part of daily life and is changing the way every professional communicates and markets. By developing a plan that incorporates best practices with a whole lot of common sense, our social media strategies will grow and evolve as quickly as social media tools change.

Who Cares About Privacy? You'd Better!

Christopher Burgess
@BurgessCT
Atiegeo, LLC

Privacy: why do we care? What if we ignored the whole topic and simply focused on the operational tasks at hand? Who would notice? What's the downside? What level of resource investment should be made? Do I need a guide? These are all legitimate questions worth addressing as you strategize and put together your tactical plan for social media/network engagement.

In the United States, the health care arena has two sets of regulations sitting front and center that warrant understanding and consideration when setting up your social media engagement: the Health Insurance Portability and Accountability Act (HIPAA) and the Health Information Technology for Economic and Clinical Heath Act (HITECH). These two acts require businesses to meet a minimum level of compliance relative to handling the personal health information (PHI) of patients. Giving short shrift to these acts puts your brand at risk. Patients who don't trust you to protect their privacy will find a provider who does protect their PHI.

Privacy discussions must be embedded at the point of ideation and design whether you're designing a patient support entity where you control the entire technological ecosystem or using a third-party infrastructure (e.g., Facebook). In either case, you should provide a guide for anyone who will be engaging with you via social media. Your guide should include basic rules of engagement (ranging from what type of information is permitted to caution about resisting a desire to overshare PHI) and a way to ensure they won't put their PHI at risk inadvertently.

And don't forget your employees, who also need a guidebook that provides the specifics about how you expect them to protect PHI for patients as well as colleagues (see: Social Media Governance for a policy database of 170+ exemplars). Count on your employees doing not only what is most efficient, but what achieves the goals and objectives. A guide helps them know exactly what you expect. You want to avoid these common pitfalls:

- Using third-party environments to collaborate on patient follow-up and care that aren't designed to protect PHI (i.e., private groups within Facebook).
- Setting up a closed patient support group that ties patient membership to their PHI (i.e., requiring patients to link to their electronic health records as part of the registration system).

- Commenting on patient-specific illness or PHI within one's social networking platforms (see: Doctor busted for patient info spill on Facebook).

My bottom-line caution: do not assume that compliance with various regulations and requirements automatically ensures security when it comes to PHI, nor is privacy automatically guaranteed.

Here's a Great Strategy: Think Sociologically

Meredith Gould, Ph.D.
@meredithgould
Digital Strategist and Communications Consultant

Here's everything you need to know about my perspective: it's sociological.

More specifically this means my observations and counsel about social media—strategy and deployment—are anchored in these basic sociological principles:

1. The word "social" refers to "group" not chit chat.
2. Every aspect of society—institutions, organizations, interactions—is socially constructed.
3. Socially constructed reality is revealed by asking, "What's going on?" and "Says who?"
4. The process by which individuals form a group, and a group then becomes a community, is a social process.
5. Social processes can be tracked, measured, and replicated.

There you have it, Sociology 101 as well as basic Social Theory and Sociological Methods in five bullet points. Moving right along...

I believe it's critically important to keep these sociological basics in mind during strategic planning sessions, especially when discussing how individuals might use social media. (Please note: individual action is an illusion, especially relative to social media.)

Go ahead and ask anyone on Twitter—I've been known to get cranky (in public) whenever I see tools being confused with strategies and social media strategies being developed without a more nuanced appreciation of "the social."

On a good day, I respectfully request (and on a bad day insist with some edginess) that health and health care social media strategists put more time and effort into understanding social context. I ask that we mindfully:

- look beyond audience or target market demographics to explore cultural nuances within and between groups *viz.* age, sex, ethnicity, religion, socio-economic status;
- pay more attention to the sociology of health (i.e., health, wellness, disease, illness) as well as the sociology of health care (i.e., industry sectors) viz. understanding the social construction and maintenance of health and health care; and

- realize that anything that happens in a "real" community will happen in the virtual communities we seek to create, as well as ones emerging organically.

Years of active participant observation in health care social media have me convinced social media offers great tools for transforming individuals into groups and groups into communities. We simply need to think more sociologically to create strategies to help make this happen—for the sake of better health and health care delivery.

A Doctor's Perspective on Social Media Strategy

Matthew S. Katz, M.D.
@subatomicdoc
Radiation Oncology Associates, PA

Social media changes the way we communicate—how we perceive and present ourselves. Because the fundamental unit of business value becomes the individual when social media is involved, organizational objectives must be designed to engage individuals. Once you know your purpose and interests, defining objectives and how to use social media strategically will flow from there.

How we interact is key to how traditional organizations function. As noted by authors of *The Cluetrain Manifesto:*

- Markets are conversations.
- Markets consist of human beings, not demographic sectors.
- Hyperlinks subvert hierarchy.
- These networked conversations are enabling powerful new forms of social organization and knowledge exchange to emerge.

Social media permits us to listen and share with others easily and instantly without geographic or social boundaries like nationality or religion. As a result, our definition of community is changing as well.

Some organizations will be challenged while others will thrive because of these new communication tools. In the United States, corporations are legally defined as individuals. As individuals fuse personal and professional aspects of life online, we may benefit from first considering a business strategy for ourselves before defining one for our organization.

Doctors, for example, organize and present themselves on social media based on how they balance interests in patient care, administrative responsibilities, research, education, and advocacy.

Doctors can develop expertise and then choose how to use that knowledge to improve patient health, thus capturing key features suggested by author Daniel Pink. In his book, *Drive*, Pink suggests effective organizations allow employees to develop autonomy, mastery, and purpose. Sometimes the training for mastery is formalized, like in medicine. But sometimes it isn't.

Engaged, motivated employees are the functional subunit of any effective organization. So define yourself and your objectives first, then decide how well that fits with your organization's objections. Only then will you be able to use social media strategically.

If you're planning strategy as the organization, then use business principles to help decide which social media tools to use. I've found Forrester Research's POST method helpful:

People: What are people ready for?
Objectives: What are your objectives?
Strategy: How do you want your relationship with others to change?
Technology: What applications/technology should you use?

Start with you. Define your values, purpose, and both personal and professional objectives. Decide whether to use social media strategically for both personal and professional objectives. You'll discover some tools work better than others.

If the formal organization you work for is prepared to start using social media, you can decide how your motivation might allow you to help that organization. If your formal organization is not ready, begin anyway based upon your purpose and values.

The ROI is Real but the Message Matters

Howard J. Luks, M.D.
@hjluks
New York Medical College
Westchester Medical Center

As Dr. Ted Eytan discovered when questioning (anonymous) physicians on Sermo, many are simply not interested in establishing an online presence. They're concerned about putting themselves at risk.

I imagine many of these same physicians have no problem using a static Web site to claim they're "the best," have a "premiere practice," and use "state-of-the-art" modalities. Ironically, their promotional language probably puts them at more risk than venturing into social media where we, as a community, have discussed risks and established ways to avoid potential problems.

And then there are physicians whose disinterest in health care social media stems from worrying about investing in something that won't yield measurable results. My experience has been very different.

The percentage of new patients (7%-10%) entering my practice because of my social media presence and information on my Web site underscores the value of investing time in these resources. Even more significantly, patients who discover me via social media and my Web site tend to arrive far better prepared and informed. They're also more comfortable with me, thanks to watching my videos. All this makes my time with them more productive and more efficient. I'm an advocate of using a blog and/or Web site to present meaningful, evidence-based content without adding any commercialized hype. Do this and patients will:

- Find you because of your digital property exposure;
- Like you, because if they don't like your videos or content they won't show up;
- Probably trust you more than a doc they found in the phone book;
- Interact with you far more efficiently since they've already digested online content—which you can revisit right then and there to reinforce what you have just told them; and
- Dramatically improve your patient satisfaction scores.

As a physician, I maintain an online presence to make trustworthy, evidence-based (when available), actionable information and guidance available to patients and consumers from around the world.

I'm not looking at my engagement from an ROI perspective. I personally believe physicians have a moral obligation to fill Google's servers with quality content to drown out the commercialized nonsense that currently exists online. But for those more focused on getting patients in the door, the message here is clear: social media works; it's only the medium and the risk is manageable.

Social Media... Operations?

Reed Smith
@reedsmith
Social Health Institute/Gray Digital Group

You already have a strategy. Maybe your strategy is to stay away from social media? Maybe it's to test the waters? Or maybe, just maybe, you'll jump in full force? In any case, it's important to understand where you are and identify your goals.

So where are you?

- What is the history of the hospital?
- Does the current culture lend itself to innovation?
- Do you have a leader who "gets" social media?
- How much of this is your sole responsibility?

These are just a few questions to get you thinking. The last thing you want to do is make things harder on yourself if there isn't a payoff of some sort at the end. I encourage you to know your landscape and be realistic about goals you set.

What about goals?

- Do you just want to get involved with social media so you can be in social media?
- Are you using social media activity to further current facility goals?
- How do you plan to measure your work?
- What are the expectations relative to results?

I hope at this point you're not discouraged. I bring all this up because many people want to know how to use a tool or platform rather than how to meet goals. I encourage you to avoid thinking about social media as a marketing strategy, although marketing is a big part.

Instead, I challenge you to look at social media in terms of operations. If you really want to engage administrators, talk about social media in their terms. How could social media help (to name a few):

- Internal communications
- Physician sales
- Shift change handoffs

- Patient discharge process
- Team building or reward and recognition programs
- Crisis communications

If your facility works or has worked with the Studer Group, the Baptist Leadership Group, or others, think about how:

- Current Baldrige criteria ask for feedback on how social media and Web-based technologies are used to listen to customers.
- Social media could have an impact on senior leader rounding.
- Discharge follow up calls could reduce readmissions.
- Social media could help your employee "bright idea" program.

In sum, do not get stuck in the rut of wanting to do social media for marketing only. Be sure you look at the bigger picture and organizational goals. You currently sit in a place at a time when you can truly make a difference with the technologies available.

Who Will Manage Your Social Media Presence?

Mark Ryan, M.D., FAAFP
@RichmondDoc
Virginia Commonwealth University School of Medicine,
Department of Family Medicine

Dedicating any time or effort toward developing and maintaining a social media presence will be unproductive unless you decide how to use it. Without taking this important first step, your social media account(s) will be somewhat aimless and probably not very useful.

Will you use social media to provide information to a general audience or a more specific group? Will you use social media to push information out to your audience, or will you be engaging in dialogue with them? Your answers to these questions will determine who will manage your social media presence and how that presence will look.

Make sure whoever manages your social media account(s) is interested in doing so and is capable. Find someone who truly wants to be involved and can take ownership of the social media presence, who will give it the time it needs, and who will engage with account friends and followers. In the world of social media, dialogue and experience develop trust and demonstrate expertise.

Also, make sure your organization's employees have access to social media accounts. Facebook, Twitter, and others are, after all, simply new ways to communicate; phones and fax machines were once innovations. Train employees to communicate responsibly and effectively, and then trust them to use their access appropriately.

Finally, make your accounts valuable and attractive by:

- Interacting with the community and audience;
- Providing added value by becoming a trusted resource for information, guidance, and so on;
- Starting slowly with the understanding that it takes time to develop an effective social media presence; and
- Being honest and engaging.

9 Ways to Change Health Care

Mary Pat Whaley
@Mary_Pat_Whaley

Health care is changing. It's changing to eliminate waste of money, time, and resources. It's changing to make more care available with fewer providers. It's changing to empower patients to participate in their own care.

How will you change with the times? Here are nine ideas:

1. Make your Web site interactive, clean-looking, interactive, friendly, and interactive. Think of your Web site as your digital receptionist. If all your patients can do on your Web site is look up your phone number, you're wasting everyone's time. Patients want to register, make appointments, pay bills, get test results, chat online with a staff member, access personal health records (PHRs), watch videos, and listen to podcasts you make or recommend. They do not want to wander around your phone tree or wait on hold.

2. Give your patients information, information, information. According to a MedTera study conducted in September 2010, 95% surveyed indicated they're looking for more comprehensive information about disease management, and 77% said they hadn't received any written information about their illness or medications directly from the physician.

3. Understand that people have different types of learning styles and offer your group information and medical information in different ways. Offer information via written and digital documents, videos, and podcasts. Offer support groups and group education for the newly diagnosed. Help patients build communities around your practice.

4. Take down all those signs asking people to turn off their cell phones. Cell phones are going to revolutionize health care, so embrace them. For all you know the person on the cellphone when you walk in the exam room is texting "gr8 visit til now, wil i <3 doc?" (Great visit until now, will I love the doctor?)

5. Eliminate the wait. Patients have much better things to do than wait. It doesn't matter why a provider is late—you're cutting into patients' ability to make money and get things done. Text them to let them know the provider is running late. Text them to let them know an earlier appointment is available. Give patients an appointment range

(between 10 am and 12 noon), then text them when their appointment is 20 minutes away.

6. Use a patient portal to take credit cards, keep them securely on file, and stop sending patients statements. Use the portal to deliver results to, chat with, and e-mail patients.

7. Stop fighting the tide and let your staff use social media at work—for work. Involve everyone in Facebook, Twitter, your Web site, and blog. Using social media for communication and marketing is not a one-person job.

8. Form a patient advisory board and listen to what specifics your patients want from you. If people don't have time to attend a face-to-face meeting, use Skype.

9. Think about alternate service delivery models, both in person (group visits, home visits) and digitally (e-mail, texting, Skype, avatar coaches, home monitoring systems). *Emotional technology* studies show people can improve health by accepting and utilizing health care technologies.

What do patients want? They want *information, communication, and a real connection with you*. Use social media and technology innovations to make it happen.

Using Social Media Strategically

Bertalan Mesko, M.D.
@Berci
Webicina.com

If you want to participate in social media to create an online presence for yourself, you should communicate clearly and openly, just like in the real, off-line world.

Social media is simply a form of communication and should not be treated as something more important. If I should come up with some suggestions about designing a social media presence, I would mention these:

- Be open to discussions.
- Communicate as you would in real life.
- Define your goals (e.g., to promote your company or create an online presence for yourself).
- Design your strategy (e.g., if you need short, fast conversations to achieve your goals, stick to Twitter; if you need an online platform to share your thoughts, essays, slideshows, etc., create and manage a blog).
- Do not mix professional and personal lives online.
- Be consistent: whatever topics you tend to cover, keep on covering them.
- Commitment is crucial: no matter how good your strategy is, if you do not commit enough time and effort to reach your goals, it just won't work.

Start by listening online. Every medical specialty and condition is already covered; there are patients and medical professionals focusing on all these topics. Go online, find these key opinion leaders and major voices, listen to what they're saying day by day, and define your strategies by using their pieces of advice.

If you have questions, feel free to ask. The vast majority of people in medicine and health care are ready to help you. You do not have to invent the wheel, ask your readers, users, or contacts when you want to find out what they need from you.

As in real life, social media is simply a form of communication. It's faster, more interactive, archivable, and interactive; but it's just communication, so do what you do in the off-line world and it's going to work.

The (New) Pediatrician's (New) Handshake

Wendy Sue Swanson, M.D.
@SeattleMamaDoc
Seattle Children's Hospital, The Everett Clinic

One of my mentors in residency told me the pediatrician's handshake was different. Instead of grasping a child's palm, pediatricians touch the top of a baby's head, feeling the fontanelle or soft spot. Often, it's one of the first things we do when we meet our new patients. As I see it, our handshake is changing again and is now different because of opportunities afforded by social media and innovative technology.

As a doctor, I firmly believe I have an obligation share my expertise and my experiences in understanding pediatrics online. Technology simply makes it easier. Medicine is far from static; being online allows me to share what I learn every week with my patients.

And my patients are online far more often than they are with me in the office, so instead of only exchanging ideas when they gown-up in exam room #4, I can join them where they already are—in social networks, on the Internet, on their smart phones, and on YouTube. The educational space extends beyond the examining room.

I also understand patients want intimate, personal, responsive, and empathetic care from doctors. All medicine can't be practiced online. To accommodate this reality, I work part time seeing patients in a traditional clinic setting and part time using tools like Twitter, my blog, LinkedIn, Doximity, and YouTube to share what I know. Or what I'm learning.

In my mind, it's obvious how technology builds a bond for my patients and for me. This isn't one-sided; rather it's bidirectional. Through social media, I feel more connected with science, with my mission to cure children, and with my patients. I give lots to technology. I get and learn far more in return. I would suspect my patients would echo this sentiment.

Technology provides these two essentials in my world as a pediatrician, mom, wife, and community member:

1. Sharing. I share thoughts about new research, new opinions, and new trends and controversies in parenting and pediatrics. I share my stumbles as a parent. Physicians share opinions all day; sharing online is arguably no different. Families in my practice (and others outside of it) can follow my online content year round and access what I think about new research or controversial parenting topics.

2. Education. I'm an educator by profession (pediatrician, former middle school teacher, mom). Innovations like Google Body allow me to use advancing technologies to demonstrate, teach, and inform families why their child is ill or in pain or how they'll heal. I send parents to my blog since it offers comprehensive detail regarding the rationale behind my recommendations. For example, why do I say no to Tylenol when kids get shots? Why do I think it's essential to keep kids rear-facing in car seats until age two? In the 15-20 minute visit I'm allowed in practice, there simply won't be time to review everything. My blog serves as a repository of my advice and where I think science holds answers to help us make great decisions for our children.

<u>Notes</u>

Section Three

Blogging

Health care Blogging: Wide-Open Opportunities

Phil Baumann, R.N.
@PhilBaumann
Health Is Social

"Blogging is dead."

I can't tell you how often I hear that. According to the Health Care Social Media List, fewer than 200 hospitals have blogs—that's less than four percent of all U.S. hospitals! Meanwhile, more than 900 hospitals have Twitter and accounts and over 1,200 have Facebook pages. Does this mean blogging is dead? Or does it mean hospitals are passing up important opportunities to communicate?

I understand why some think blogging is dead. More and more people are turning to Twitter and other real-time media to publish and interact. Also, resources are scarce. A tweet is 140 characters. It's Twitter. Can it get any easier? *"Why blog when you can tweet? Attention spans are short anyway."*

My clients report their agencies have told them Web sites are basically useless; Twitter, Facebook, and YouTube are all that's needed anymore; blogging wasn't worth the effort and nobody reads blogs.

Nobody reads blogs?

Well, Google does. Google loves blogs. Don't you think Google is an important "follower"? Which would you rather have—10,000 followers on Twitter, 99.9% of whom ignore your tweets? Or a search engine, like Google, that indexes and archives your blog's content and then serves it up to anyone actively looking for what you might have to say?

Patients read blogs too.

"Oh, we tried a blog, but only had 25 subscribers."

Only 25? Well, what if a few of those readers were health care journalists, philanthropists, or patients connected via their own communication platforms to thousands of others? And what if you have only one subscriber but your content helps her lead a better life, even if in some small way? Would you characterize her as "only" one?

Twitter, Facebook, and other streaming media have created the illusion that longer-form content doesn't matter much anymore. Actually, where do you think all that good stuff people share on Twitter and Facebook comes from? Blogs.

These three things must be integrated to build an audience: content, context, and process. Content and context provide relevance—a no-brainer. You need process to deliver relevance. If you have none of the skills required for blogging, then you won't understand how to develop and execute the processes needed to properly execute your strategies. It's that simple. Blogging is a skill involving more than just putting up content—it's a process.

In today's world, your interactions do have to be swift, which is also a skill best honed by the experience of blogging. I'm not saying you need a blog—I am saying you need the underlying skills. Blogging is a great way to cultivate them.

Blogging Gives Patients Freedom of the Press— and That's Freedom to Be Heard

Dave deBronkart
@ePatientDave

American journalist A. J. Liebling famously said, "Freedom of the press is guaranteed only to those who own one." Blogging gives you one.

It's not just a happy metaphor, either. A generation ago the only way to get your thoughts to a wider audience was through broadcast or print, and the only way to do that was with big capital equipment. To be heard, you had to go through people who had that capital. They had to bless your words, or you couldn't get at their equipment. With a blog, the only resource you need is computer access. Profound. Not only do you not need permission: *you can say anything you want.*

Blogs are free and public. They sprinkle ideas like seeds in soil: some never take root, but some do and sprout, and some of those sprouts grow tall. Some get noticed and some don't, but that doesn't hold you back: *you can express whatever you want.*

Consider what happened to me.

I started a blog because I'd beaten a usually fatal cancer. (Good enough.) I wrote whatever I felt like, ranging from thanking my doctors to ranting about statistics and touting my hobby (barbershop singing). Then I got interested in health care and wrote about that but not that much.

But in 2009, I wrote about my medical records, and in less than a month it bent federal policy. I'd discovered my insurance billing history was a mess, and unbeknownst to me, the post stomped in a mud puddle of policy being discussed in Washington. Twelve days later it was on the front page of the newspaper. Pretty soon the proposed policy was ditched—because of one middle-aged guy from New Hampshire, in a recliner New Hampshire just writing what he was thinking.

I didn't even *try* to do this, but blogging generated invitations to federal policy meetings, and invitations to speak at conferences to doctors, patients, and policy people. Who knew?

Perhaps you're like Amy Tenderich of DiabetesMine, who simply wanted to connect with others to discuss her condition. Or, you're like Kelly Young of RAWarrior.com, who started writing about her condition and soon attracted thousands of followers. You might be like Robin Smith and her friends in the Cushing's community, who discovered each other across vast distances. Each of these patient blogs was started by someone who initially had no idea whether anyone would listen and then discovered that many would—and did.

What's on your mind that you'd like to express? Even if nobody's listening? Go for it; someone might.

Humanize Your Hospital by Blogging

Dan Hinmon
@hivedan
Hive Strategies

In Search of Excellence author and renowned business consultant Tom Peters says,

> "No single thing in the last fifteen years professionally has been more important to my life than blogging. It has changed my life. It has changed my perspective. It has changed my emotional outlook. And it's the best marketing tool by an order of magnitude I have ever had."

Despite that ringing endorsement, of the 1,501 hospitals engaged in social media, only 185 host blogs, according to the Health Care Social Media List. All those other hospitals are missing out on a huge opportunity.

Your hospital should be blogging to:

- Build loyal relationships with your community. Regularly blogging useful, interesting information practically guarantees that readers will return to your Web site again and again.
- Humanize your organization. Blogging adds a personal touch to your hospital Web site that a list of services simply can't. See what Dr. Wendy Sue Swanson, has done for Seattle Children's Hospital on her blog, Seattle Mama Doc.
- Give your leadership, staff, patients, and community members a voice. Anna Roth, CEO of Contra Costa Regional Medical, provides a great example on her blog, Doing Common Things Uncommonly Well .
- Boost your Google rankings. Google search loves Web sites with fresh information, and blogging is a powerful way to accomplish that.

So with all these great opportunities, why do so many hospitals hesitate to blog?

Blogging requires more thought and preparation than short Facebook posts or tweets on Twitter, and to be successful, you need to post a blog at least once a week. Posting two or three times a week is even more effective. Add blogging to a lengthy list of daily tasks, and it can easily seem overwhelming.

Here are four ways to make blogging easier for you and your organization:

- Develop an editorial calendar and stick to it.
- Recruit a team of bloggers: CEOs, dietitians, educators, nurses, pharmacists, cancer survivors, new moms, board members, donors, grateful patients. They're all possible blog writers, although they will probably need to be edited by an editorial services professional.
- Keep your posts short—under 400 words—and to the point. Readers will appreciate it.
- Don't worry about writing a masterpiece each time. Just do it.

Some useful tips:

- Be friendly, conversational, and interesting.
- Write with patients and caregivers in mind. You're not trying to write to everybody. You're trying to write to somebody who will view your hospital as the go-to place for medical care.
- Avoid technical jargon and medical speak like the plague!
- Don't be discouraged if you feel no one is reading your blog. It will take some time to build readership. People will find you if you consistently post something useful and interesting.
- Make sure you offer an RSS feed so you're easy to follow.

As an added bonus, a hospital blog is the perfect place to update your staff, the community, and media during times of breaking news, emergency, or natural disaster.

Tom Peters is right. I have found that nothing helps me organize and clarify my thinking better than blogging. Try it, stick with it, and you'll like it.

Why Blogging Matters for Physicians

Mike Sevilla, M.D.

@drmikesevilla

Patients seem to be highlighting the value of social media for physicians and providers. Every day patients bring in printouts from Internet sites and ask me what I think. What if I tell you that patients can learn about you and about how you care for them, even before meeting you? How? The answer is blogging. Physicians can get a lot of mileage out of blogging in the areas of marketing, patient education, and commentary.

Marketing: Lots of newspaper ads announced my arrival to the community when I started working in my small town of Salem, Ohio in 2001. I also delivered lots of talks at local community organizations to achieve more name and face recognition. In today's world, new physicians are writing blog posts and using other social media platforms (which are more cost effective, i.e., free) to introduce themselves to the community. I can tell you that in the past year, I've had more and more new patients tell me that I was selected because they enjoyed my social media presence. Patients enjoy the TV interviews that I post on my Web site. In addition, patients state that they enjoy the informational blog posts on medical topics like flu shots and chronic disease care.

Patient education: When it comes to clinical care, colleagues tell me all the time, "Ten to fifteen times a day, I tell patients why I don't think they need an antibiotic." Do you have clinical tips or topics that you frequently discuss during your workday? For example, do you spend too much time dispelling myths perpetuated on television or on less-than-reputable Internet sites? What if you wrote a blog post about that topic, including evidence-based information, and then directed patients to it? What if you recorded a You-Tube video about a clinical topic that patients could watch on a smart-phone while waiting for you in the exam room? Mayo Clinic does this very well.

Commentary: Kevin Pho, M.D., is the leading voice in physician blogging. He began his blog in 2004, not to become famous but because his patients asked him to respond to medical hot topics. For him, it was easier to place his thoughts about important issues in a blog post and refer patients to it so he could more easily focus on the patient care visit while getting his point of view across to the community.

I blog at my Web site, Family Medicine Rocks, to write about advocacy issues, especially those involving family medicine and health policy. For example, I wrote a blog post when there was another threat for Medicare physician payment cuts. The response was overwhelming. Visits to my blog tripled for two days as this post was retweeted and posted on other sites. Not only have blogging and other social media tools given me opportunities to share my point of view with a larger audience, but they have also made it possible to become an opinion leader in my specialty relative to advocacy.

What are you passionate about? What are things you say each and every day to patients, to families, and to colleagues? I bet you have some thoughts about how we can make this broken health care system better. I challenge you to write down all those ideas right now. This is your first step in the blogging process.

Health Care Blogging is Alive and Well

Christian Sinclair, M.D.
@ctsinclair
Gentiva Health Services

Some have declared blogs dead in the age of short-form communication platforms like Twitter, but if you really look closely, many tweets and Facebook posts link to longer-form content.

Blogs will always have a prominent role in the social media tool kit for health care professionals. Blogging encourages versatility by offering options for embeddable content and remixing different media to create an impact more powerful than using text alone. The challenge is always being entertaining enough to keep readers interested but thoughtful enough to show that you're making salient points about complex medical issues.

As a health care blogger you'll need to choose your target audience and aim the content to the right level. After all, there's a reason you won't see shoppers picking up the latest *Journal of American Medical Association* for an easy read. But you can still access and engage the public by taking the topics from an issue of JAMA and writing about how they may affect your clinical practice.

Health care blogging can put forward different types of voices, but the one I find the most helpful is what I term the *approachable professional*—friendly, engaging, conversational. You can find this voice by remembering the last time you went to dinner with clinicians and nonclinicians. The most satisfying conversation for all is when everyone is involved and no one feels alienated by lack of education or experience. This is the voice of an approachable professional and one of the more effective techniques in health care social media for several reasons.

By blogging as an approachable professional, you establish yourself as a learned professional; one who actually reads the primary literature and not just *USA Today* headlines about medical research. This establishes trust and confidence in the clinical reader (because they don't all read the stacks of journals on their desks) and the nonclinical reader (who expects you to read all the stacks of journals on your desk).

Go ahead and add data or the scientific explanations to give your posts credibility but then review what you've written. Before going live, review your post to ensure that you've presented that information in a way that would appeal to that mixed company at dinner. If the approachable tone is there, you're finished. If it isn't, go back and take out convoluted sentences and jargon. Consider using metaphor to explain a complex process. You might start your post with a story reflecting the dilemma at hand. These are all simple ways to become an approachable professional, practically guaranteeing your online stock will rise and you'll make a difference in the world beyond your clinic doors.

Notes

Section Four

Social Networking

Connecting the (People) Dots Using LinkedIn

Andre Blackman
@mindofandre
Pulse+Signal

Social media platforms, such as Facebook and Twitter, make it easy to find people, to allow people to find you, and to get into conversation. LinkedIn is one platform that focuses on fostering such much-needed interactions for business professionals. You won't find videos of dancing cats on this social network—it's "strictly business." What you will find is a dynamic platform where people share credentials and professional accomplishments and discover potential colleagues.

Launched in 2003, LinkedIn now has over 135 million users in over 200 countries. The question for you as a health care professional is this: is LinkedIn useful for you as an individual and for your organization? In short, the answer is yes.

For Health Care Professionals

Remember when you would find job listings on Web sites and hit "apply" if interested? Well, those days are still here, but LinkedIn makes it possible to discover who in your network might already be connected to the organization or individual you're trying to reach.

Finding a great gig isn't the only benefit of LinkedIn participation. I've used this social networking site to help me research innovative health organizations to profile on my blog or how to get in touch with someone I've read about. For example, when I wanted to learn more about members of a panel session I'd be speaking with on global health innovation, I went straight to LinkedIn and did my homework on their expertise. Doing this led me to see how we were already connected through a number of mutual colleagues. And that inspired other ways to opportunities to collaborate beyond the conference.

Already been to a conference and met some great people, or maybe getting ready to attend one? Rather than meticulously keeping business cards stacked somewhere, find those new colleagues on LinkedIn and invite them to connect. Voilá! Your own digital Rolodex!

For Health Care Organizations

LinkedIn offers opportunities for organizations to be listed and to post updates about initiatives and achievements. For example, the American Cancer Society (ACS) is an organization you can search for on LinkedIn, but ACS doesn't stop there. They also integrate fresh news and resources as well as recent blog posts. LinkedIn allows organizations to integrate other social content, providing another way to showcase open positions, engage with potential employees and clients or customers.

LinkedIn also provides ways for employees to get involved in professional groups. Using LinkedIn's rich search function, you'll find plenty of health care focused groups with relevant resources and discussions (e.g., American Public Health Association, #HCSM (health communications & social media), Connected Health Community, Health 2.0).

Another useful tool is LinkedIn's Q&A area, simply called "Answers." Drilling down into the topic area of health care uncovers questions from LinkedIn members. Provide answers on behalf of your organization to establish or increased credibility and expertise.

Whether you're using it as a solo health care professional—and yes, there are health care practitioners on LinkedIn—or on behalf of your organization, LinkedIn is definitely something worthy of your full attention because it's an investment in your professional future. And when I say future, think about this: you never know what you'll need, until you need it.

Building Relationships on YouTube

Susanna French
@susannafrench
Dartmouth-Hitchcock

Our four most-viewed videos are not the compelling patient stories most likely to end up shared on Facebook or talked about over dinner. They're didactic talking-head videos with hand surgeons about rare conditions and traumas—and they make up half our channel's traffic.

Lots of people, it turns out, seek medical advice on YouTube. We pour good resources into our Web site, and I spend hours every week on our Facebook page, but neither venue gets anywhere near the mail our YouTube channel does. Virtually all our channel's comments and direct messages are about these four conditions. These patients are looking for advice from us.

Before they searched for this information, they probably didn't know us from lonelygirl15. But there's so little available on these conditions, and our videos present real people who clearly know exactly what these patients are going through. As a result, visitors feel comfortable asking, "Should I have the surgery?" "Do you think it's broken?" or, "Should I have someone look at it?" Some simply want us to reply with phone numbers and directions.

They could get this information by visiting our Web site, but choose to post comments and wait for our reply. Replying with the information they request goes a long way toward building the relationships that were the impetus for our starting the channel in the first place.

As it would be unethical and irresponsible to offer medical advice, my ever-present challenge is finding new ways to answer the same question over and over without looking like I'm cutting and pasting. Our most popular video has elicited dozens of virtually identical comments. Of course, patients are not identical. They are, however, in pain and desperate enough to seek help from strangers, so they deserve my most thoughtful, helpful reply within the confines of my role as YouTube administrator.

If they want information that may be useful to other viewers, I'll forward the comment to the doctor who was in the video, and post the reply. Mostly, they want our advice, and that's where I have to keep urging them to get checked out in person because we can't diagnose without an exam.

Our channel is changing as we cultivate our fledgling social media program. Until recently, it's been a repository of marketing content: patient stories, provider interviews, location tours, and event coverage. Seeking deeper engagement with our audiences on the social level, we're now learning how to add videos on the fly in ways better suited to the space: more often, more diverse, less formal. It's a natural shift, given how viewers are using content. We'll be bringing more providers to our channel more frequently in different ways, such as with video extras we've added to our podcast series.

People seek help in familiar places. They're used to the tone and format of forums like Facebook and YouTube. Meeting them there, as opposed to the howling uncertainty of the larger Internet, can be a great service to someone in pain. I think of it as a virtual house call.

I often get messages that end, as a recent one did, "I am desperate." As professionals bridging the space between the provider and the patient, we can use the ubiquity of YouTube to reach ever-wider audiences—not so that we can coat the virtual world with our brands, but so we can get help for those who haven't found it yet.

And I know it makes a difference. One woman said of her son, "After watching your video, I think he may have childhood absence epilepsy." Another viewer said, "This video gives me hope, Thank you." Measure *that* ROI.

Pinterest for Health is a Beautiful Thing... Literally

Meredith Gould, Ph.D.
@meredithgould
Digital Strategist and Communications Consultant

From zero to gazillion miles per hour in weeks—that's how quickly Pinterest, the latest social media platform, has caught on. First adopted by artists, photographers, crafters, and do-it-yourselfers, Pinterest has swiftly captured the attention of marketers across industries.

Still, I note a bit of head-scratching among health care social media enthusiasts who are busy asking: How could Pinterest be used to generate business and patient engagement? What sorts of content should we be pinning? What sorts of boards should we be creating? What are we to do in the absence of categories for health or medicine?

Great questions, but from my (multiple identity) perspective as an artist, e-Patient, and caregiver, I say there's nothing wrong—and a lot that's very wise—with simply focusing on this existing category: **art**. I say it's worth considering the incalculable value of pinning images that can soothe mind and spirit while the body is under siege. I suggest we start asking how Pinterest might be used to enhance someone's healing process.

Sites like CaringBridge and CarePages make it possible for loved ones to deliver ongoing encouragement for patients and caregivers. Now, imagine using Pinterest boards (individual or shared) to enhance mood and outlook for self and others.

Here are some examples from my own self-soothing account: irises (paintings and drawings of my all-time favorite flower that will last longer than real irises ever do) and inspired healing (images that remind me that while we may not be cured, we can always be healed).

I visit the boards titled "fractals" and "microscopic" to remember there's beauty to be found in the natural sciences, something that really helps when I'm feeling disgusted with all thing medical.

If laughter is the best medicine, can beauty be far behind? Hopefully not.

Health Care Videos Go Beyond *Marcus Welby* and *House*

Aldon Hynes
@ahynes1
Community Health Center, Inc.

If a picture is worth a thousand words, then a 30-second video clip at 30 frames per second must be worth nearly a million. It's not really quite that simple, but it's close. Online videos are a powerful way to easily reach your audience. From public service announcements to patient education, online video is one way to spread essential public health information and empower patients as well as providers.

Consider these additional benefits: Some people simply learn better from videos than they do from reading text. Others who might not want to take the time to read a blog post, will make time to watch a short video. And because videos provide opportunities for engagement and humor, they've become one of the most popular forms of content for users to share with friends.

At the Community Health Center in Connecticut, which provides primary care to underserved populations, we use online videos to let people know about our programs and celebrate important milestones of community life. Dartmouth-Hitchcock has used videos to explain social media policies to staff in a humorous and memorable way. Mayo Clinic uses videos to raise health awareness and a growing number of health care organizations are using videos for advocacy efforts. We even got supporters to create video for us by sponsoring a contest! Elementary school students around the country submitted videos about how they thought kids could fight obesity and helped share our message to their friends.

While YouTube immediately comes to mind, opportunities for sharing video online include Facebook videos as well as established platforms like Vimeo and Blip.TV. You can use services to live stream video, like Ustream. TV, JustIn.TV and Livestream.com. Other systems, like Qik focus, make it possible to stream videos from mobile devices and integrate nicely with larger video sites.

Production options have expanded in recent years. Smartphones are often used for quick live videos, and recently a director shot a full length film using a smartphone. Numerous other devices, such as digital cameras and DSLRs make it possible to shoot great video. Tools like iMovie or Movie Maker allow you to stitch together pictures and audio, either music or recordings, to make simple yet effective videos. Once you're satisfied with the results, you can also use online video sites, like YouTube, Facebook, and others, to distribute your videos.

Consider branching into animation, which might be a particularly good choice for patient education videos. XtraNormal is now integrated with YouTube so you can easily create an animated video using text-to-speech. Educational animated videos can be produced in a few minutes, but as with any production, the more time you put into it, the better the result is likely to be.

The truly creative, or those looking for an excuse to play video games at work, might even want to explore machinima (creating animated videos using video games). Experienced machinimatographers put together scripts for their video game actors, arrange the camera shots, sometimes from multiple angles, and then do a screen capture of the video game and post produce the video.

Personal motion capture devices are on the horizon. These devices capture the movement of actors and can be used to create animated videos that more closely reflect the desired motions of the characters.

Capturing the attention and imagination of providers and patients alike is always a challenge. Fortunately, many tools for creating and sharing online videos are free. They're also so simple to understand and so easy to use that that even small health care organizations can make a big difference with video.

Facebook Forces Us Into the Conversations We Should Have Been Having All Along

Cynthia Floyd Manley
@CynthiaManley
Vanderbilt University Medical Center

The oncologist was so angry he was shaking.

How had his photo ended up on Facebook? Why was the Cancer Center even on Facebook? "No good can come of this. I want no part of it. The only people who will post are gonna be pissed off."

Ok, my bad. He'd been caught off guard when a patient casually mentioned he'd seen Dr. X's photo on our Facebook page. Even if it was the same photo on the Cancer Center's Web site, I know better than to let a doctor be caught off guard.

I checked his photo and found two comments: "Dr. X is the best urologic oncologist in the galaxy," and "Thank you, Dr. X, for saving my husband's life." I let Dr. X know about the comments, "which I have deleted at your request."

We got into Facebook two and a half years ago. Since then, I can count on one hand the negative postings we've had on our page.

I'm not suggesting there aren't risks in having a Facebook page for your hospital. I'm saying that, in my experience, the benefits far outweigh the risks, and the risks can be managed with some thought and research.

The most obvious benefit is being where your patients, families, and prospects are every single day. Increasingly, if you aren't there, you might as well not exist.

Done right, Facebook lets you put a human face on your organization. You can teach and inform. You can learn what your customers need, want, and expect. And you can listen to word of mouth, accelerate the positive through meaningful engagement, and mitigate the negative.

One example stands out. A woman whose father was dying of pancreatic cancer posted a complaint about their oncologist by name. I took the conversation off-line by messaging her directly in Facebook. I apologized that she felt disrespected by the doctor and promised to share her comments with the doctor (which I did).

We exchanged a few messages. She thanked me for responding and apologized if she'd been too harsh. I realized that she was a devastated daughter who just wanted to be heard and to have some control over a crappy situation. Two weeks later, she posted that her father had died and thanked our team for doing all we could to save him and to ease his suffering when we could not.

Had we not been on Facebook, odds are she would have complained on her own page. Friends and family would have jumped in, all would have been left with a bad impression of us, and we wouldn't have even known it. Instead, we neutralized the situation. But more importantly, I hope that by reaching out to her, I helped ease her own suffering a tiny bit.

Facebook, and social networking platforms like it, are not just unavoidable necessities. By forcing us into the genuine conversations we should have been having with our patients and families all along, social media can help us be better health care providers.

A postscript: Dr. X is no longer with us. A PR colleague at his current hospital tells me he has become quite the social media darling. Imagine.

Changing Health Care 140 Characters at a Time

Dana M. Lewis
@DanaMLewis
#hcsm | Swedish

If you've read the title of this piece and scoffed, you're in good company. Almost everyone in health care scoffs the first time I talk about Twitter.

You can scoff, but you'd better keep your ears open because it's true: individuals on Twitter are changing health care.

In 2008, I started talking to others on Twitter about health and social media. I quickly realized lack of resources wasn't the only reason many organizations weren't using these new tools. Fear and uncertainty were also in the mix. I also spotted this pattern during one-on-one conversations, so I decided to have a conversation with three people. Others clamored to join. I then thought I'd try this newfangled "hashtag" (#) so that we could track our conversation on Twitter.

Thus, #hcsm was born.

What started as a one-time conversation turned into a weekly chat on Sundays at 8:00 pm CT. The chat has turned into a community engaging every type of health care organization imaginable: small, large, local, international, medical device, pharmaceuticals, nonprofits, patient organizations, health systems, and more. A wide range of individuals participate: physicians, nurses, patients, lawyers, patient advocates, caregivers, communication professionals, etc.

The power of the chat—and Twitter—is rooted in connections within this community.

Patients begin to see the story behind the "endless waits" in waiting rooms, learn about their disease, and find others like them. Physicians learn how patients find information online and why social media is so valuable. Health care professionals educate the general public. Organizations learn from each other about what works and what doesn't on Facebook, Twitter, YouTube, and other networks. And individuals from all these groups start crafting solutions together to solve today's health care problems.

And yes, it all happens in 140-character nuggets of insight.

I'm often asked about Twitter chats in greater detail because I moderate the largest (and original) health care chat. Best practices: 1) make sure there's a community you're passionate about building and 2) establish clear rules for participation.

Whether it's a #hcsm geo-chat (a chat specific to a country or region, a la #hcsmEU) or a specific health chat (i.e., #dsma, which focuses on diabetes), a one-time chat or a regularly occurring chat, you need:

- *People to moderate.* (This can be the same person, or you can rotate)
- *People to chat.* Is this a new community? Do you need to tap into existing communities (get permission!) to spread the word about your chat, or just announce it to your existing community?
- *Established format.* Do you want the moderator to keep everyone on topic, or do you want it to be 'open mic'?
- *Clear rules.* Communicate these often as you establish the chat or community.

For example, the only rules for the weekly #hcsm chat are

- Stay on topic
- Don't shamelessly self-promote during the #hcsm hour (because it's not about you)
- Have fun!

The last #hcsm rule is possibly the most important in our community because #hcsm gathers some of the brightest minds in health care (including you) to talk about all things health and social media and improving health care—and we have fun while we do it. Want to join? Just add the hashtag (#hcsm) to your tweets and join in anytime.

"Hi, my Name is Crohn's and I Have Jill Disease … Facebook me?"

Jill M. Plevinsky
@jillplev
Boston Children's Hospital

No need to bore you with the statistics, because if you're reading this you most likely already know that Facebook is where it's at, so to speak. So if "everyone" is on it, and we know just about "everyone" will have a health problem at some point, we can safely assume people will rally around health conversations as much as they rally around their favorite American Idol contestant. (Just like me, Casey Abrams is someone with inflammatory bowel disease [IBD]).

I was diagnosed with Crohn's disease at age seven in 1995. I signed up for a Facebook profile in 2006. By that time, I'd already established myself as an empowered patient within the IBD community thanks to some motherly nudging and support from the local chapter of the Crohn's and Colitis Foundation of America.

Having Crohn's disease was a part of my identity. I felt weird meeting a new person and knowing they weren't aware of my diagnosis. I'd find ways to work it into the conversation. For example, "Oh, does that have nuts in it? I can't eat nuts, I have Crohn's disease." It wasn't to elicit any particular reaction; I just wanted everyone to know. And so, as is the case with any other information I wanted everyone to know in this digital age, I put it online. More specifically, on Facebook.

I once posted a status that featured a whiny complaint about having a busy day, being super exhausted, and my stomach bothering me sprinkled with a little profanity (look, I was 19, I know better now) and placing the blame on "my Crohn's." Within hours my post had generated comments and wall posts from friends with and without IBD with encouraging words and understanding. Pow! Insta–social support, even if they had no idea what I was actually experiencing.

Clusters of patients gather on Facebook groups and pages specific to their particular illness. They do this because they know their audience shares their experience. Within these communities, complaints are met with both sympathy and advice, resources, and personal stories. Most of these Facebook groups have built membership simply by choosing a catchy name and keeping active. These pages are more attractive than a plain old forum with an unfamiliar format and are free from the awkwardness of showing up at a support group. And they actually help—the patients, that is.

Facebook clearly helps patients help themselves. But can it help patients help providers?

I administer a Facebook group of approximately fifteen adolescent and young-adult patients with IBD who are the Patient Advisory Council (PAC) for ImproveCareNow, supported by the C3N Project. Pediatric physicians affiliated with these collaboratives have a vested interest in what their patients think about the care they deliver. The PAC uses the Facebook group to provide feedback that helps the physicians and developers create innovations that they'll actually use. Pow again! Insta–focus group.

I wouldn't call it a "support community" per se, but since when do all patient communities need to be all support all the time? Patient groups are also developing around calls to action that span across specific health issues. You'll find most of them are on Facebook.

Twitter and the World of Personalized Medicine

Robert W. West, Jr., Ph.D.

@westr

SUNY Upstate Medical University

While the historical progression of social media may have transitioned from blogs to Facebook to Twitter, I recommend starting with Twitter (via TweetDeck, where you can monitor multiple columns of tweet sources). Your initial goal would be to identify the most credible sources of information on a particular topic area (e.g., health care social media or #hcsm) and follow conversations there.

Start with just a few people (e.g., @westr) or venues (#hcsm) and you'll see how by following the streams, and then "following" other people (tweeps) or venues (e.g., #bcsm, #meded, or #rheum), how quickly you can amplify your information stream.

For me, one of the biggest benefits Twitter offers is access, via hypertext link, to original journal articles, respectable magazine or newspaper articles, blogs and Web-only sources of information (e.g., WebMD). Now, after using Twitter for about 18 months, I rely on it as my primary source of daily professional information.

Of course, Twitter can double as a source of personal information if you wish to include that as part of your information stream. Since you compose your information stream to suit your particular interests (e.g., "e-Patient"), it ends up becoming a network of interrelated themes that can be modified according to your daily needs.

As a professor at a medical school, one of my goals is to train budding physicians in the use of social media because that's where abundant medical information is available. Just as importantly, that's where patients are!

To this end, I implement such training in an elective called Personalized Medicine 101, as well as via yearly "Twitter Tutorial" talks available to the Upstate Med community at large. Through additional speaking venues, I attempt to teach others about the impact of social media, including established physicians in our geographical community (see: Female physicians on Twitter), and fellow e-patients in our virtual community (see: Fibromuscular Dysplasia blog by Kari Ulrich, RN).

Since the majority of my Twitter use involves exchanging information for pedagogical purposes, and since Twitter does not maintain a running archive of tweets (only up to one week or so), I obtain backup support through a Web program called BackupMy.Net. A description of this service and its value was published at SMHN in May of 2011.

The beauty of Twitter involves its range of capabilities. Because Twitter is as easy as you want to make it and as complex and powerful as you could want it to be, it's difficult to get bored. In fact, beware, Twitter can be addictive!

Twitter Chats Build Community

Colleen Young
@colleen_young | *@VirtualHospice*
Health Care Social Media (#hcsmca) | Canadian Virtual Hospice

A Twitter chat, like many things, is relatively easy to start. However, building relationships and sustaining the community requires time and effort. The groundwork for success must be laid well in advance.

First ask yourself: Does the world need another health care chat? What's your niche? For #hcsmca (health care social media Canada), it was a question of local vs. global. Participating regularly in #hcsm (health care social media) and #hcsmeu (health care social media European Union) chats led me to contemplate whether there was an appetite to share locally as an adjunct to the global conversation. As Neil Crump states, "Social chat and the Web are global, but regulations, culture, and the way health is paid for create segments of similarity where it makes sense to focus discussion."

When I was considering starting #hcsmca during the summer of 2010, I interviewed founders of existing successful health care chats (e.g., #hcsm, #hpm, #nhssm, #hcsmeu) to help me understand what I was getting into. I wanted to know

- What is the workload for the founder of a Twitter chat?
- What were the motivations and goals for each Twitter group?
- What were their best practices?

Today, there are Twitter chats on an amazingly wide range of health-related topics. But if you want to start a new one, first follow chats you like, ask for advice from founders and build on their experience. I learned these key points:

Start your community before your first chat.
Contact people in your online and off-line networks to ensure people come to the first chat. Choose people who will set the tone you wish to establish. These founding members can help you determine the optimal time and day for your chat, suggest topics, and generate activity and awareness.

Create a home base.
Twitter doesn't archive well. To capture the community's history, establish a home base. I write community-related articles, introduce or summarize some of the chats, and make announcements (such as meet-up plans) on my blog. I use a Google spreadsheet to let participants submit topics and to archive the transcripts.

Continue establishing meaningful connections and building relationships.

Get to know participants and potential participants. I reach out to people who may be interested in #hcsmca and who may not have participated before. When a topic is submitted, I invite subject matter experts to join the chat. Increasingly, I rely on lists to get to know people.

I used TweetDeck to make lists of people who have used the hashtag #hcsmca and people interested in Canadian health care who have not used the hashtag. When I see people with common interests, I connect them. If someone has a query that interests the community, I invite them to submit a chat topic.

Collaborating and networking beyond community membership broadens the community's knowledge and expands access to resources.

Be prepared to commit, but also learn to share the load.

While moderators experience rewards, it takes time and effort to host a weekly chat and maintain relationships beyond the chats. Eileen O'Brien (#socpharm) warned me about this. I took her sage advice and introduced guest moderators from the beginning. Guest moderators expand the network, contribute to the relationship building, and bring different perspectives and styles that enrich the community.

Moderating isn't the only way community members can help. Some may contribute by promoting the community to colleagues or at conferences, announcing upcoming chats regularly, welcoming newcomers during chats, or organizing meet-ups. Identify these members and thank them for their support. Recognizing the value of their contribution encourages them to continue and others to follow suit.

Why Twitter? Because of its near real-time functioning, Twitter can help you stay current, expand your network, crowd-source ideas, and learn, learn, learn. Chats help filter Twitter for stuff that's relevant to you.

Building a Facebook Community? Keep Calm and Carry On!

Kelly Young
@rawarrior
Rheumatoid Patient Foundation

I could write (and have written) lists of tips for using a Facebook page successfully for health topics. But, the most essential principle I can share about my success on Facebook is a philosophical one. If you use social media in an authentic and reliable way, then you already have the secret weapon.

Maybe it's because Kelly means "warrior," but I love how the 1939 World War II poster *Keep Calm and Carry On* sums up working with social media. It's an absolutely indispensible philosophy on Facebook, especially when the topic is health. Distraction, detractors, and disturbances will occur, but you must keep calm and carry on with your mission.

Keeping calm means being authentic as you respond to individual people, not just reacting to situations. If you are honest, kind, and generous with your words, a community will grow reflecting that atmosphere. People are drawn to pages with authentic leaders and members.

Even when a post is opposing or insulting, you can respond in a genuine way:

- Acknowledge the other person's point of view.
- Respond factually or offer links pages presenting facts on the matter.
- Agree with something if you can, and admit it's alright to disagree.
- Politely state that spam and personal attacks not allowed. And delete them.

Carry On means focusing on your mission to meet the needs of this community. Remaining focused no matter what was something I learned growing up in a U.S. Marine Corps household. A group will grow and prosper in social media, as anywhere else, when people's needs are being met, so focus on that!

A variety of people, none with exactly the same viewpoint, will post on a public page. Your determination, in your role as page administrator or community manager, to address needs is what will bring everyone together to form a community. Whether it's Facebook's repeated updates or changes in your industry itself, some kind nuisance will always present itself, but you must carry on. You'll succeed if you adjusting to changes while remaining faithful to the mission.

Even when something interferes with your goals, your page can remain reliable by:

- Providing worthwhile, relevant topics for discussion.
- Regularly posting fresh material from your own or another trusted Web site.
- Doing the hard work of finding useful information not easily accessible elsewhere.
- Sharing about the importance of the common mission.

Working on public social media platforms like Facebook with topics as personal as health can be challenging, which is probably why many don't attempt it. Slick marketing always produces some effect, so many rely upon that. But if your goal is bringing together people who trust your organization, you'll need more than marketing gimmicks. You'll need to learn how to keep calm and carry on so you can serve people and focus on ways your organization can meet their needs.

Appendix A:

Keeping It Legal

Daniel Goldman, J.D.
@daniel280
Mayo Clinic

What Are the Unique Challenges of Social Media?

Speed

If information moves at light speed on the Internet, it moves at light speed x10 within social networks because of their interconnected nature.

You simply do not have time to think, react, and control situations arising in social media the way you do with traditional media, or even on static Internet pages a few people see.

Reach

Many individuals have expansive social networks with thousands of friends on Facebook, and hundreds, thousands, or even millions of followers on Twitter. Top videos on YouTube are viewed *millions* of times. If Lady GaGa is a patient at your hospital and has a bad experience, then decides to say "tweet it," that message will be received by *14 million* followers.

Blurring of Professional and Public

Social media is about sharing what's going on, and for most people this includes all aspects of life. Most social media sites encourage participants to provide and display information about where they work.

The very nature of social media makes it difficult to segment life enough to distinguish between professional and private endeavors, something that creates all sorts of challenges for organizations and the professional reputations of employees.

For example, if a nurse at your hospital posts pictures of weekend off-duty drinking exploits on Facebook, what impact will that have on your hospital's reputation if it's on the same page as discussions of day-to-day work responsibilities?

A Generation of "Lifecasters"

Those under the age of 25, "digital natives," who have grown up with social media have a very different view of privacy than older cohorts. This generation of "lifecasters" is comfortable broadcasting every aspect of their life on the Internet with large groups of people—many of whom they know tangentially or have never met. Managing this new paradigm for privacy is an enormous challenge.

What's Unique About Health Care Social Media?

Privacy

HIPAA and state privacy laws make social media particularly challenging for health care organizations. These strict privacy requirements mean high stakes if employees act inappropriately while using social media. Violations of patient privacy, whether intentional or inadvertent, can lead to liability under HIPAA and state privacy laws and to enormous PR ramifications.

Privacy laws may also limit your ability to engage in social media dialogue and may prevent you from defending your company online. If you're a car manufacturer and someone posts on their Facebook page that your car was defective and caused an accident, you can respond on their Facebook page (or your own). But if you're a health care provider and someone posts on your Facebook page that your hospital committed malpractice when you treated them, you'd generally be prevented by HIPAA and state privacy laws from defending yourself, since it would invariably require you to disclose the patient's PHI.

Practice of Medicine Issues

The nature of social media (personal interaction, dialogue, etc.) means there's an increased risk that providers will unintentionally be seen as practicing medicine or otherwise providing care to patients or prospective patients. This can lead to malpractice claims and could raise licensure issues if the "patient" is located in a state where the provider is not licensed. Twitter raises the additional risk that its short character limit makes it more difficult to provide any meaningful disclaimers regarding this issue.

Ethical Issues of Medical Professionals
Becoming Social Media "Friends" With Patients

Is it ever appropriate for a health care provider to become social media "friends" with a patient on their non–work-related social media platforms? This question can raise challenging issues regarding appropriate boundaries for the treating relationship, especially for mental health professionals.

Drafting Your Company's Social Media Policy

There's No "One Size Fits All"

Social media policies are as much a reflection of corporate culture as they are a reflection of legal requirements. To draft an effective social media policy, you must understand your company's brand as well as tolerance for dissent and risk and then balance these with what the law allows.

Social Media Is a Dialogue, Not a Monologue

You need to understand differences between social media and traditional marketing communications. Traditional marketing communications, which include advertising, are typically one-way channels that impart information to others. Social media is a conversation. The expectation is that others will talk back *and you will listen.*

Lawyers naturally want to control everything and remove anything that we or our clients don't like or that is risky. If your company intends to use social media with that attitude, they will not succeed.

While you don't need to tolerate defamatory or unlawful material, you do need to be willing to live with valid criticism. The community of users expects that you'll react to such criticism by communicating and attempting to make the situation better, not by removing negative information or other activities that smack of "censorship."

If your company is uncomfortable with accepting and responding to criticism in a public forum, social media may not be for you. But opting out really isn't an option because even if you choose not to participate in social media, others will still talk about you.

You Cannot Control Social Media, But You Can Effectively Manage It

The unique aspects of social media noted above (i.e., speed, reach, etc.) mean that you cannot control social media the way you can control traditional media. Even if your company elects to block all social media on company systems, you cannot completely control what employees do during off hours or on their mobile devices.

You cannot control what other people say about your company, although you may have some recourse if people say anything untruthful or defamatory. What you can do is effectively manage social media by crafting clear and reasonable polices, communicating them to employees, and making reasonable efforts to monitor what's said about you online.

Education and Awareness Are Crucial

The best policy in the world is useless if employees are unaware of it or don't understand how it applies to their actions. Once you've drafted policy, make sure that it's communicated to employees and is easily accessible. Consider making it available online and publicly available so employees can access it during off hours or at home when they're most likely to be accessing social media and wondering, "Is it really ok to say that on Facebook?"

Even more importantly, make efforts to educate employees about the policy and how it applies in specific situations. For example, translating complex privacy regulations like HIPAA into online situations isn't always intuitive, so providing concrete examples and training about what is and isn't permissible is crucial. Consider adding social media training into new employee orientation and yearly compliance education.

Expect... and Plan for... a Crisis

No matter how well-drafted your policy and how well-educated your workforce, there's always the potential for a crisis. Because of issues discussed above (i.e., speed, reach, etc.) these issues can become major public relations disasters in almost no time.

The recent social media crisis experienced by Domino's Pizza (YouTube video posted by employees showing employees tainting the food) is a prime example. Identify your crisis management team ahead of time and, even more importantly, have a plan for managing a crisis (e.g., privacy breach, irate customer spewing venom, etc.) before it happens. Time is of the essence when dealing with a social media crisis. If you do not react quickly, troublesome material may be seen by thousands or millions before you have a chance to react.

Borrow From Others to Develop Your Policy

Lots of companies have given this issue a lot of thought. Reviewing policies from similar organizations will help you ferret out the issues important to your company and provide ideas about how to handle challenging issues. Particularly good policy examples are those from Intel, Sun Microsystems, and IBM.

Specific Issues to Consider Addressing in Your Policy

Communicate your company's stance about employee use of social media during work time. Philosophies about this run the gamut from blocking and prohibiting all social media sites at work, to actively encouraging employees to use social media on the theory they'll be "brand ambassadors."

Consider what your company's position is on this issue and communicate it to employees. Often the issue can be addressed with reference to existing company policies prohibiting nonwork activities on company time.

Identify Who Can Speak on Behalf of the Company

Let employees know who is authorized to officially speak on behalf of the company on social media. Often this will be designated employees in your public relations department. Be clear that employees must refrain from making it appear as if they're speaking on behalf of the company or communicating your company's official position on issues if they're not authorized to do so.

Address the "Blurring" Issue Head-on

Many states regulate employers' attempts to discipline lawful off-duty conduct of employees, so you may not be able to tell employees they may not discuss their drinking exploits or strip club visit on Facebook. However, you can remind employees that if they're going to engage in activities that are incompatible with your company's brand or public image, they should not identify themselves as employees of your company on social media.

Along the same lines, you should consider requiring employees to add a disclaimer to their social media posts or sites indicating they're speaking on their own behalf, not your company's.

Note: Tread carefully if your policy addresses critical comments. The National Labor Relations Act protects an employees' rights to collectively discuss wages, hours, and working conditions. The National Labor Relations Board (NLRB) has been active in this area and filed complaints against companies it believes are inappropriately chilling an employee's right to collectively discuss these protected issues.

The NLRB takes the position that any social media posts which can be construed as comments about wages, hours, or working conditions and are either discussed with other employees or are targeted to an audience that includes other employees, are protected "concerted activity" under the NLRA.

"Maliciously false" statements by employees are not protected, as are mere "individual gripes." The NLRB has also filed complaints against companies whose social media policies are, in the NLRB's opinion, overly broad in that they prohibit all social media comments about the company without acknowledging the employees' rights to discuss wages, hours and working conditions under the NLRA. The law is developing quickly in this area, with new cases coming out every week, so you talk with legal counsel before drafting policy or disciplining an employee for comments made about your company through social media.

Stress the Importance of Maintaining Patient/Customer Privacy

The speed and ease with which people can make social media posts and a life-casting mentality combine to make privacy a very dangerous area. This is a particular concern in an industry such as health care where there are not only significant customer expectations but also a challenging regulatory environment (e.g., HIPAA, state privacy laws, FDA).

Health care provides a prime example of what can happen when employees do not fully understand and adhere to their obligations in this area.

There have been numerous cases over the last few years of health care employees posting pictures and other protected health information of patients to social media platforms. Some have been for nefarious purposes that would not have been prevented by policies, but others have been through inattention to the rules or a fundamental misunderstanding about how the law applies to social media. It's important that any social media policy clearly and unequivocally communicate how employees are expected to maintain customer privacy and business confidentiality just as they would on-site or in any other non–virtual venue.

Perhaps more importantly, social media policies should provide examples of behavior that violate the policy, especially in the non-obvious situations. For example, in health care, employees may think that because they've removed the patient's name from their blog posts about a baby they delivered, there's no HIPAA violation. However, have they really removed all information that might make the patient identifiable under HIPAA? Especially in small communities or with respect to unique medical conditions, there just might be enough identifiers to make the information identifiable.

Separate and apart from the issue of whether discussing customers violates privacy regulations, address the issue of appropriate professional behavior. Is it ever appropriate for doctors and nurses to be discuss de-identified patient interactions online, particularly if the tone is negative or critical?

I'm reminded of a tweet I read that was sent by a physician who spoke derisively of an overweight diabetic patient who refused to change his eating habits. While the information was completely de-identified and therefore did not violate any privacy laws, it was unprofessional and cast him and his employer in a negative light. Consider reminding employees that professionalism and courtesy toward customers are, in many ways, just as important as legal privacy requirements.

Stress the Importance of Maintaining Business Confidentiality

Remind employees that they must maintain confidentiality about trade secrets and other confidential business information and should not discuss information online.

Prohibit Employees From Speaking Anonymously or Pseudonymously About Your Company

Speaking anonymously or pseudonymously is considered dishonest and unethical behavior in the social media world and, if discovered, will lead to negative publicity. It can also lead to legal liability because the FTC considers the employment relationship to be a "material connection" that must be disclosed by anyone endorsing or recommending a product or service (see more detailed discussion of the FTC guides below).

If employees send a tweet to all followers recommending your company's products or services and do not disclose they work for your company, you could be subject to an FTC enforcement action. You must specifically address this issue in your policy because the FTC has stated on a number of occasions that if there's a violation, they'll deal less harshly with those companies that have policies in place and inform employees of requirements.

FTC Endorsement and Testimonial Guidelines (16 CFR 255)

http://www.ftc.gov/os/2009/10/091005revisedendorsementguides.pdf

These have been around forever and generally prohibit deceptive advertising practices in connection with endorsements and testimonials.

The guidelines were significantly revamped in October 2009 and now specifically address social media. Review and address them in your policy. In particular, note that anyone endorsing a product must disclose any "material connection," which includes any compensation in connection with the endorsement. This would include giving the endorser free samples to conduct the review. It also means that employees who "endorse" their organization's products or services must disclose their employment relationship. Guidelines should make clear that employees should disclose their relationship to your company if discussing your company or its products or services.

Restrictions on Lobbying and Political Activity

If your company is tax-exempt, make sure your policy addresses restrictions on lobbying and political activity. IRS regulations prohibit tax-exempt organizations from supporting candidates in campaigns and broadly restrict most other political activity by exempt organizations. Make sure policies address this issue and ensure that those participating in social media on your company's behalf or in ways that could be imputed to your company, understand the rules.

Harassment of Other Employees

Employees invariably talk to and about each other in social media spaces. Remind them to be civil and comply with existing policies about treatment of colleagues, non-harassment, and respect in the workplace.

Intellectual Property

Make sure your social media team understands what they can and can't do with the intellectual property of others. Posting or reposting information by others without permission can lead to infringement claims against your company.

False Advertising

Make sure your social media team understands rules about false advertising and what they can—and cannot—say about your own products and services, and about the products and services of competitors. The informality of the medium plus its ease and speed can lead to disparaging posts about competitors or unsubstantiated claims about your own company that could generate a claim of false advertising.

Notes

Appendix B:

Planning Your Strategic Framework

Strategic Framework for Social Media

This document provides a framework with key elements that should be included in any well-designed social media plan. Answering the following questions will help you think through the issues.

Business Goals

- [ ] What business outcome do you want to support or problem do you need to solve?
- [ ] Who are the key stakeholders or community members (aka, "the audience")?
- [ ] Is your audience comprised of individuals, small groups, or formal organizations?
- [ ] What do you know about your audience?
- [ ] What demographic mix must you consider?
- [ ] What general and health literacy levels are present?
- [ ] How can social media tools be deployed to help you better understand your audience?

Desired Outcomes

- [ ] What do you want to change through your proposed initiative?
- [ ] Is that change on the individual, small-group, or formal organizational level?
- [ ] What do you want your audience to know/believe about your organization?
- [ ] How do you want them to feel?
- [ ] What action(s) do you want them to take?
- [ ] Are those actions individual or collective?

Choosing Tools

- [ ] Which platforms could be most effective for connecting with your audience?
- [ ] Are you accounting for literacy levels and learning styles?
- [ ] How can social media tools coordinate with, support, and enrich existing traditional means of communication?
- [ ] Will video be helpful?
- [ ] How in-depth would interactions need to be?
- [ ] Is the subject matter too complex for video?
- [ ] Are potential community members already gathering on a particular platform?

□ How deeply do those platforms penetrate your audience?
□ Is your project sufficiently compelling that it could inspire online community members to try a new platform?
□ Must your online community be exclusive, or may anyone have access to materials and discussions?

Measurement

□ How will you judge/evaluate the success of your campaign?
□ How will you measure behavioral change?
□ How will you measure attitudinal change?
□ What actions taken by your audience will indicate successfully achieving your goal?
□ Are there intermediate goals you could measure along the path to your ultimate goal?
□ Can you convert any outcomes to a financial figure, such as increased revenue or decreased costs, so you could calculate ROI?

Format for Plan

The following elements should be included in any plan:

□ Executive Summary
□ Background/Situation Analysis
□ Business Goals and Defining Success
□ Integration of Social Media Tools with Traditional Means
□ Resources Required
□ Timeline for Implementation
□ Budget
□ Measurement
□ Conclusion

Notes

Contributors

Lee Aase is the Director of the Mayo Clinic Center for Social Media. By night, he is Chancellor of Social Media University Global (SMUG), a free online higher education institution that provides practical, hands-on training in social media for lifelong learners. Visit social-media-university-global.org.

Patricia F. Anderson is the Emerging Technologies Librarian at the University of Michigan, previously senior author of a reference work on e-health information seeking for patients.

Phil Baumann is a registered nurse who helps health care professionals leverage technology for better care. Visit: HealthIsSocial.com.

Ed Bennett manages the University of Maryland Medical System Web program, is founder of the Hospital Social Network List, and has a special interest in employee-access to social media.

Andre Blackman is a connected agent of change in health innovation at pulseandsignal.com and cofounder of the. fastforwardhealth.org.

Christopher Boyer is Director of Digital Marketing and Communications for Inova Health System and a nationally recognized advocate for the fiscally responsible use of social media. Visit: Christopher Boyer.

Christopher Burgess is C.O.O. and Chief Security Officer at Atigeo, LLC. Co-author of *Secrets Stolen, Fortunes Lost: Preventing Intellectual Property Theft and Economic Espionage in the 21st Century*.

Dave deBronkart has led online communities since CompuServe in 1989. Favorite socmed advice: "Just be *useful*, will ya?? And charming wouldn't hurt." Visit: e-PatientDave.

Susanna French writes and handles social media for the dartmouth-hitchcock. org health system in northern New England.

Meredith Gould, Ph.D. is a sociologist who provides digital strategy and communications consulting services to mission-based organizations. She's also the author of eight books. Visit: meredithgould.com

Dan Hinmon is principal of Hive Strategies, a firm providing webinars, workshops, and consulting to help health care systems build online patient communities.

Shel Holtz counsels organizations on communicating effectively, particularly with digital technology. The author of six books, he is also a blogger and podcaster. Visit: Holz Communications + Technology.

Aldon Hynes has used media socially since sharing coloring books in kindergarten. He now works as the Social Media Manager for the Community Health Center, Inc.

Matthew S. Katz, M.D., is a partner in Radiation Oncology Associates, PA and Medical Director of Radiation Oncology at Lowell General Hospital in Lowell, Massachusetts.

Dana Lewis is the interactive marketing specialist for swedish.org, where she develops and implements social and digital health strategies. She's also the founder and moderator of healthsocmed.com.

Howard Luks, M.D., is a social media–savvy orthopedist fascinated by the potential impact of social and mobile media on content delivery and care. Information subverts hierarchy. Visit: www.howardluksmd.com

Cynthia Floyd Manley is a content strategist and social marketer for a major academic medical center in Nashville, Tenn. She's worked twenty years in PR and marketing, but is always a journalist at heart.

Bertalan Mesko, M.D., is managing director of Webicina.com and author of ScienceRoll. He teaches social media at the University of Debrecen Medical School and Health Science Center.

Jill M. Plevinsky is a 20-something researcher, e-patient, and community-builder dedicated to improving lives of youth with inflammatory bowel disease. Visit: jillplev.tumblr.com.

Mark Ryan, M.D., F.A.A.F.P., teaches medical students, works with medically underserved communities, and leads global health projects while blogging at A Life in Underserved Medicine and Social Media Health care: Community of Practice.

Mike Sevilla, M.D., is a Family Physician in Salem, Ohio. He is founder of the Family Medicine Rocks Web site, including TV interviews and podcasts.

Christian Sinclair, M.D., F.A.A.H.P.M., is a palliative medicine physician based in Overland Park, KS, and serves as editor of Pallimed.

Reed Smith is a consulting strategist and thought leader focused on integrating social computing into hospitals and how technology can improve patient experience. Visit: Reed Smith.

Wendy Sue Swanson, M.D., M.B.E, F.A.A.P, is a pediatrician, mother, author, and speaker. She's marrying stories with scientific evidence to improve partnerships in health care. Visit: SeattleMamaDoc™

Farris Timimi, M.D., is a Mayo Clinic cardiologist who serves as the Medical Director for the Mayo Clinic Center for Social Media. He also is the Program director for Mayo Clinic's Advanced Heart Failure Transplant Cardiology Fellowship Program.

Mary Pat Whaley is a consultant, author, and speaker who provides health care managers, executives, and providers with advice, resources, and information to drive organizational excellence via Manage My Practice.

Robert West, Ph.D., is a molecular biologist, geneticist, professor, course director, advisory dean, ardent e-Patient, personalized medicine evangelist, and chronic pain sufferer. Visit: Personalized Medicine 101.

Colleen Young is the Founder of #hcsmca and Community Manager of Canadian Virtual Hospice. She's a community builder who listens, connects, informs, and constantly learns.

Kelly Young is a writer, speaker, and patient advocate working to empower patients and improve care. She created rawarrior.com and founded the nonprofit Rheumatoid Patient Foundation.

Afterword

Join us in the Revolution!

We hope that reading Bringing the *Social Media Revolution to Health Care* has inspired you, and you see why it's crucial that we who are concerned about health care and serving patients need to use social media tools to improve health care, promote health, and fight disease.

These essays have been about the *what* and *why* of health care social media—the timeless reasons for involvement. Through the Mayo Clinic Center for Social Media, we also have resources to help with specifics of the *who*, *when* and *how*.

We invite you to take a closer look at our resources and to visit http://social media.mayoclinic.org on a regular basis to find updated news and information. Please feel free to contact us via email at: socialmediacenter@mayo.edu.

For the Revolution,

Lee Aase
Director

Farris Timimi, M.D.
Medical Director

Social Media Health Network

The Social Media Health Network (SMHN), a service of the Mayo Clinic Center for Social Media, provides access to tools, resources and guidance for organizations and individuals interested in using social media for health and health care.

Membership dues are based on the size of the organization as reflected in annual revenue. Membership benefits include:

- full access for all employees to the Social Media Health Network community site, which features discussion forums, training materials (including archived webinars), and other resources.
- free or reduced registration for conferences and other training and networking opportunities, such as:
  - The annual Social Media Summit and preconference workshops held each October at Mayo Clinic in Rochester, Minn.
  - Regional conferences produced with local collaborators. If you are interested in hosting and co-producing a conference, please contact us!
  - Social Media Residency—a hands-on, in-depth course.
- member-only events, including in-person member meetings and conference calls.
- free source code or low-cost hosting for blogs or community sites.
- community support for blogs and community platforms.

Social Media Health Network memberships also are available for individuals.

For more information about SMHN, or to request a membership application, call: 507-538-0492 or contact us via email: socialmediacenter@mayo.edu

Social Media Residency

Others offer social media "bootcamps," but the Mayo Clinic Center for Social Media uses a medical metaphor to more accurately convey the nature of our most intense social media training program.

Just as medical residency is more advanced than medical school, Social Media Residency offers more than social media basics. Still, it's accessible for motivated beginners who want to accelerate learning.

To meet a broad spectrum of needs we've designed curriculum that includes pre-requisites and a quick self-study preparation program to help novices gain initial experience. We also provide resources for social media residents to connect and learn from each other before, during, and after the on-campus program.

We maintain a resident/faculty ratio of no greater than 8:1 to facilitate and ensure interactive learning. We use experienced mentors (a.k.a. Chief Residents) drawn from our staff and External Advisory Board or Internal Advisory Group members.

Our first priority: creating a dynamic learning experience. To this end, our Residency offers a mix of didactic, small group and hands-on pedagogy—learning tools by using tools. Some online training takes place in "safe spaces" where beginners can feel free to experiment, but we also require participation in public hands-on activities using online social platforms to develop comfort and confidence.

Upon completion of Social Media Residency, participants will be able to:

- apply Social Media (Twitter, Facebook, YouTube, Blogging) best practices in their organization;
- select which social media tools are most appropriate for their organization;
- identify components of an appropriate social media strategy;
- explain how social media tools can help improve their organization;
- recognize ways social media can help improve patient and employee communications;
- analyze ways social media can improve patient and provider education; and
- demonstrate how to shoot videos with a pocket camcorder and other video cameras and equipment.

Social Media Fellows Program

To encourage more meaningful adoption of social media tools and deepen the pool of advocates and advisors within Mayo Clinic and elsewhere, the Mayo Clinic Center for Social Media offers a Social Media Fellows program. Advancement for Fellows is tied to education about social media, community involvement, successfully completing practical projects, and publishing research findings on social media in health and health care.

Our primary goal is to provide a pathway that encourages Mayo Clinic employees to receive social media training and then to apply it in their work. The Fellows program provides a next step after completing Social Media Residency. As with other Center for Social Media projects, the program is available to non-Mayo Clinic participants through the Social Media Health Network.

Go to http://socialmedia.mayoclinic.org for more information, or contact MCCSM via email: socialmediacenter@mayo.edu.

The Mayo Clinic Center for Social Media

The Mayo Clinic Center for Social Media (MCCSM) exists to improve health globally by accelerating effective application of social media tools throughout Mayo Clinic and spurring broader and deeper engagement in social media by hospitals, medical professionals and patients.

The Social Media Health Network (SMHN), a service of MCCSM, provides access to tools, resources and guidance for organizations and individuals wanting to apply social media in health and health care. For information on joining, visit: http://socialmedia.mayoclinic.org/network/joining/

29408919R00065

Made in the USA
Lexington, KY
24 January 2014